THEBLONDS

THEBLONDS

Glamour Fashion Fantasy

RIZZOLI
NEW YORK

FOREWORD
by Daphne Guinness
7

BLONDS ON BLONDS
9

NO BUSINESS
LIKE SHOW
21

LEGENDARY OPULENCE

by Billy Porter

149

SHOOTING STARS

153

MAKING MAGIC

249

The Blonds come from a real place, which stems from the club scene surrounding the late Andy Warhol. As designers, they employ a freedom of expression and a flair for the fantastical. Their collections are intelligent and the narrative of all of it comes from their soul. The Blonds don't bow to trends and their vision feels right because it comes from a place of music, books, and film; their references and narratives are fascinating.

I have always loved wearing designs from The Blonds; the pieces feel like they're from another dimension: otherworldly, dazzling, commanding, sculpted. That said, they are comfortable and easy to move within. Perfect for performance.

Our connection started, unbeknownst to any of us, when I wore one of their catsuits in my David LaChapelle music video for "Evening in Space." That suit met the transcendental tone of the film so well, and it fit like a glove. But our collaboration really began when I met David and Phillipe through our mutual friend Joe Lally. He had been working with them on an art film, and that project ended up bleeding into my music video for the track "Electric Consciousness." I just fell in love with their clothes and was immediately transfixed by them. We became friends, and they asked me to walk in their 2018 show (pages 80–81). I performed one of my tracks, "Riot." It was a huge compliment to be asked, and we proved a great creative partnership. I admit it was nerve-wracking, but David and Phillipe made me feel so at ease. The energy at that show was vital and infectious—such fun to be a part of. We haven't looked back.

Since then, when visualizing my videos, I imagine how the designs of The Blonds will complete the mood and wider aesthetic: their work always enhances or perfects the idea. The clothes are so creative, so appealing: they entrance. David and Phillipe have been kind enough to let me borrow designs for myriad shoots, and they also make custom pieces for me on occasion. As well as possessing an avant-garde spirit, they are so easy to collaborate with: intuitive, generous of spirit, and genuine perfectionists.

High fashion and costume design are absolutely art forms: clothing made well has the potential to provoke, emote, communicate, and transform. It could be said that fashion has an additional weapon at its disposal: clothes directly impact the wearer's confidence, and therefore change not only our appearance, but our behavior. Great designers can change the way we look at ourselves, and thus our very culture. The Blonds are a soaring example of this. They are pioneers.

The Blonds live and breathe their designs. The way they construct things is impressive. Everything comes from them—a small but really excellent team. If you look at the interior of their designs, you see that their attention to detail is incredible. The stitching is as good as anything I've seen in Paris couture. The linings are beautiful and, in my view, real luxury, which is so rare these days. The Blonds create true fantasy wear. David and Phillipe are so open minded and graceful. I'm just happy The Blonds exist. I hope I'll be working with them for a long time.

Foreword by Daphne Guinness

Blonds on Blonds

The Blonds were born out of a desire to make their clients feel strong, confident, and powerful. Since the formation of the brand in 2006, Phillipe and David Blond have created an intricate and glamorously rebellious array of one-of-a-kind garments, catering to an extensive celebrity clientele that includes Madonna, Beyoncé, Jennifer Lopez, Rihanna, and Katy Perry. In addition, The Blonds offer this unique custom atelier experience to private clients across the globe. The Blonds are best known for their craftsmanship and a diverse use of luxury materials juxtaposed with hardware such as spikes, chains, and crystals.

As Phillipe explains it, The Blonds met "one amazing night out in New York City! That night I ditched my senior prom and headed to the Roxy with my best friend, Olys, in tow. Then David and I spotted each other from across the room. The connection was instant, like we'd known each other forever." David, who was with friends from the ballet, assumed Phillipe was a dancer. He remembers every detail of Phillipe's look: "A sheer tank top hand stitched with crystals, distressed lace, pearls, and wildly blonde streaked hair resembling something out of a fairytale. It was magic!"

Immediately they joined forces and began creating their own looks. "At the time nightlife was a breeding ground for creativity and self-expression, because there was no Instagram!" says Phillipe. David calls those early experiments predating the brand "seeds" that the pair planted by experimenting on themselves and on friends. An explosion of fun, fashion, glamour, and sparkle ensued, and today it seems The Blonds have lived many lives together—as personalities, creatives, designers, surrealists, entertainers, and, above all, partners in life.

The golden age of film, music, art, and animation are core inspirations. These elements have been ingrained in their minds for as long as they can remember and make up the DNA of The Blonds brand.

It's only natural that a pair of designers who bonded over hand-stitched crystals share a maniacal obsession with glamour and sparkle. Their message: Even too much is never enough! The Blonds are all about inclusivity, and the duo have always shared a core belief that everyone should be able to have fun with fashion and be glamorous. The Blonds brand and this book are a celebration of that, and a sign of David and Phillipe's commitment to not only dressing but entertaining their clients as well as the public and providing an escape from the everyday.

A rose by any other name

Why "The Blonds"? Phillipe recalls, "We were going through one of our many blonde moments. At the time we were bleaching our hair and emulating the legendary blondes of Hollywood, along with characters we love from the 1980s, like Barbie and Madison in *Splash*. Walking through the city we were stunned by a gallery window display of giant Warhol paintings of Barbie, and it clicked: 'The Blonds!" Still, you don't have to be flaxen-haired to be Blond, both insist. Blond, in their usage, is meant to be a state of mind. David says, "Blond is a lifestyle, an attitude, a strong look."

While Phillipe and David's connection and the name of their brand are clear, to some there is still mystery around what they create. The Blonds have been called everything from fashion, art, and artifice to costumes or couture. In their own terms, they are a custom costuming and special occasion atelier. A study of the intersection between costume and fashion, they see themselves as interpreters for their clients and strive to realize anything those clients can dream up.

"Style is something that does not have a definition," cautions Phillipe, while David says, "Style is fluid like gender or any other outward expression. Clothes are not just meant to be practical, and we don't think of our work in those terms. We prefer to create freely and live in the moment."

When David and Phillipe met, fashion and costume hadn't crossed paths in popular culture for a while. The idea of costume-level fashion was actually dismissed at the time. David says, "When we started, no one was doing anything like this. It provoked a conversation and even shocked most people! Some said, 'That's crazy,' and even, 'Who would wear that?' Now there are many new and established designers who cater to this area of the industry." With no small thanks to Phillipe and David—and the help of a few rock stars—the niche they created for themselves has blossomed into an industry of its own.

An interesting thing about performance costumes is that they must be built to last. The stage is a place where function and durability meet fashion and fantasy. A costume isn't just an eye-catching look—it requires the highest level of materials and construction available. Phillipe says, "People have a tendency to forget that the core of what we do is custom-made for performance. These pieces are special, and they must tell a story." That kind of quality is as much a part of the aesthetic as the over-the-top style needed to make an impact.

The Blonds often say that they have so much fun working that it never feels like a job, and they try not to take anything too seriously. They've never really been interested in being "traditional" fashion designers—their work is done with a tongue-in cheek-attitude. Per Phillipe, "If you don't get it, tough titty said the kitty!" But they do take garment construction and durability very seriously. They are extremely hands-on and perfectionists when it come to the

details. Whatever is needed, they will get it done "by hook crook, thread, glue, or even a screw!" as David puts it.

Phillipe and David say fashion was all they ever wanted to do. As children, they'd take whatever was around them and make it wearable and fabulous, turning T-shirts into dresses and towels into capes or tresses. "Sometimes we laugh when thinking about getting into trouble at school for constantly daydreaming as kids. Our imaginations were a safe space for us then," recalls David. Pretending to be Wonder Woman or Jem is where the dream began for them

They lived strikingly parallel lives in their early years. Both were born on islands, Phillipe in Puerto Rico and David in Key West. Islands tend to be dramatic—even the weather is extreme. The rhythms and the colors of their lives a children are still with them. Both also had relatives who shaped their trajectories. "We would be nothing without the love and support of our parents. They motivated and encouraged us to do what made us happy," says David.

Phillipe made his way to Manhattan at the age of fou and began practicing the creative arts by the time he reached middle school. His father molded the core of hi inspiration by introducing him to New York City with al its music, theater, and art. He taught him how to sew a a very young age, encouraging every creative whim and instilling the belief that anything was possible! Phillipe spent time at various art schools and internships, taking freelance jobs in fashion design and makeup as an artis before founding The Blonds.

David's relationship with his grandmother, Stella, was close and formative. On occasion he got the chance to assist her as she expressed her creativity through painting, sewing and baking magnificently elaborate cakes. She had a bold personality and a flair for the dramatic, which apparently rubbed off. David pursued a career in fashion and afte studying fashion design and merchandising, he worked fo various luxury retailers creating window displays. Shortly after meeting Phillipe, they created The Blonds.

Their Signature:
the MOST
OUTRAGEOUS
Jeweled
corsets,
each on a
perfect
confection
sparkling
like a
Diamond!
— Patrick
McDonald

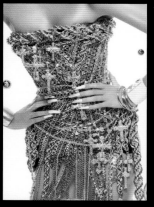

The Blonds love New York. "The city is ingrained in our brand's DNA," Phillipe says. "No day in New York is ever the same; it's like sensory overload," David adds.

The Blonds would not exist without New York—it's an endless source of inspiration and energy, and a literal source of materials. In the beginning, they scoured the many secondhand shops and vintage stores of Manhattan to get inspired by discovering unusual finds or materials. Along the way they picked up everything from antique lace and jewelry components to denim. They then created pieces as a sort of mélange, juxtaposing hardware and soft goods arranged in fantastical patterns. They have used virtually any kind of objet trouvé you can name: beads, paint, crystals, chains, spikes, and even seashells!

When The Blonds were first going out in New York, Susanne Bartsch was one individual who celebrated them. Bartsch has always championed expression and supported members of the young creative community who come together at her events. David says, "Susanne Bartsch is a fashion superhero!" These parties were a fabulous haven and the experience started at the door, where Kenny Kenny and Connie Girl ruled.

How did it start? Phillipe remembers, "There was a turning point in our career, and the catalyst was Patricia Field. She loved our looks and gave us the opportunity that changed everything by asking us to expand on a piece I was wearing at the time and turn it into a capsule collection. She featured the pieces in her SoHo store windows at Hotel Venus. We are so grateful to Pat, as she has played a huge role in our development as a brand and supported us throughout this incredible journey."

On one of their many excursions in the city, The Blonds happened upon what they refer to as, the "Perfect fucking shoe!" Upon meeting Christian Louboutin, the designers connected on every level, as Phillipe explains, "We love and live in Louboutins." Their partnership grew from The Blonds' first real runway show to every presentation since. David continues, "Our collaborations are always inspiring, whether it's a show or for a client's look, because no one creates like Louboutin."

Cut to meeting Billy Porter. David recalls, "Participating in The Met Gala was something we never thought possible, since the red carpet is rarely inclusive." However, on the day Porter arrived wearing their creation, a *Vogue.com* headline read, "Billy Porter Just Made the Most Fabulous Entrance in Met Gala History." Phillipe says, "Working with Billy is an electrifying experience. We're not only friends—we are huge fans of his work, his energy, drive, and passion. He gives life to what we do and strive to say through our work. The Met Gala carpet was one of our proudest moments, because there was a message within the walk! It was camp, queer, and, above all, showed the next generation of LGBTQIA+ that you can be whatever you want to be and still succeed in this industry."

Blond Inspiration

Together, Phillipe and David have recreated almost every fantasy they've ever dreamt up! Themes arrive from a diverse array of sources: The eighteenth century, cartoons, bondage, mythological creatures, goddesses, superheroes, burlesque, and early music videos on MTV.

The list of Hollywood icons both adore is long: Marilyn Monroe, Marlene Dietrich, Josephine Baker, Rita Hayworth, and Carmen Miranda, just to name a few. "We love the bombshells! However, the villains are our favorite, and usually the most complex and interesting characters in a book, film, or real life. I even consider myself one on occasion!" says Phillipe. Both worship the costume designers of the "Golden Age," such as Edith Head, Travilla, and Adrian. David says, "Growing up it was all about Bob Mackie's designs on the *Cher* show, *Carol Burnett*, and *Wonder Woman*." The movies they've seen, such as *Ziegfeld Follies*, made an indelible impression on them. Phillipe was starstruck by Jessica Rabbit's entrance in *Who Framed Roger Rabbit* and Michelle Pfeiffer as Catwoman in Tim Burton's *Batman Returns*, as well as the fashion show scenes in *The Women* (1939) and *Mahogany* (1975), starring the legendary Diana Ross, who designed the costumes herself.

David professes his admiration for directors such as Pedro Almodóvar, Quentin Tarantino, Billy Wilder, Baz Luhrmann, Ridley Scott, and John Waters. He adds, "We're really into fantasy, science fiction, horror, and gore films by Hitchcock, Kubrick, and Argento as well." Phillipe continues, "We're also into animation. I grew up on shows like *Jem and the Holograms*, and *She-Ra*, as well as Tim Burton and Disney films, of course, where everything sparkled, and anything was possible!"

Visual artists like Salvador Dalí, Frida Kahlo, and Andy Warhol have all influenced The Blonds. A perfect modern example of this is their ongoing collaboration with Daphne Guinness. "Our creative partnership developed into an intimate friendship, becoming almost lyrical in nature, as we practically finish each other's thoughts. Daphne is an artist—one who understands the craftsmanship and passion it takes to realize these pieces. She is the epitome of high fashion with an extremely discerning eye and razor sharp style; she is widely considered the embodiment of couture. Daphne Guinness is one of the only beings in the world with the divine ability to wear our garments effortlessly and elevate them to an alternate universe!" Phillipe exclaims, "She possesses this amazing way of transporting us with her magical visual and musical creations."

Music is another source of inspiration, and that industry has allowed them the opportunity to create for a living. David says, "We love being a part of those moments when the volume is turned up." They feed on the emotion

music conveys and love a wide variety, from pop to reggaeton, rap, and beyond. They have created costumes for many larger-than-life entertainers, and, needless to say, that has been an adventure. Phillipe says, "Music is the ultimate outlet when working on a concert, video, or tour."

The corset silhouette is the centerpiece of every collection and the house signature—the framework within which David and Phillipe start each season. David says, "Quite simply, it is the perfect foundation and the best way to shape the body by holding everything in place when layering or building out multiple changes." Depending on the performance, the structure and the strength of the corset or bustier will change. Zippers, Velcro, elastics, snaps, or buttons may be used to attach the various extensions or keep embellishments in place.

Beyoncé wore the first diamond corset The Blonds ever created in the music video for "Upgrade U." "Her amazing stylist Ty Hunter was searching for garments that reflected wealth, luxury, and glamour. Our heads exploded when that video came out and Beyoncé was wrapped in diamonds! This was another turning point, and needless to say it was definitely an upgrade!" Phillipe explains. Shortly afterward the floodgates opened, and celebrity stylists and editors poured in to request custom looks. Ty Hunter says, "I've been working with The Blonds for over a decade! I know when I need a standout piece, I can call on them." Having the opportunity to dress Beyoncé still feels like a dream! David says, "We are very thankful to have so many moments like this to celebrate!"

runway madness

The Blonds don't do traditional runway, and with each show the duo inject a heavy dose of fun into New York Fashion Week. David and Phillipe have never subscribed to seasonal rules and view their collections as a bit like great films—timeless.

"Our shows are unconventional. They're more like theater, taking the audience on a journey," says David. Phillipe adds, "What we do has really become a sort of performance art. We strive to create memorable experiences, and working with partners like MADE and IMG has made it possible to take these moments to the next level." The narrative for a collection typically blends something beautiful and sweet with something twisted and surreal. David says, "We use narratives, real or imagined, to come up with the themes or looks for a show. Having an epic story to tell makes producing these events more interesting. We enjoy mixing elements to create a paradox."

In some cases, The Blonds are asked to insert narratives into the world of fashion. NBCUniversal approached the brand to partner during Fall/Winter 2017 fashion week to promote its new Tom Cruise film, *The Mummy*. For other shows the inspiration is less direct, and more lyrical. The Blonds' Spring/Summer 2018 show interpreted the lush and descriptive language of Samuel Taylor Coleridge's "Kubla Khan" to explore the idea of Xanadu through imagery from Phillipe and David's island childhoods. Reflective materials added shine to outfits in electric colors that resembled birds of paradise. Tropical flowers and plants were also woven through the show: models wore hibiscus in their hair and in painted patterns. The aim was to use color judiciously so that it was only one part of the story—comparable to just one of the many images that make up Coleridge's fantastical poem, or the lyric of a favorite song.

A signature of each show is the reveal (pages 16–17): "With a fashion show you have to make a statement within minutes. Reveals always add that extra bit of anticipation, drama, and excitement to a show. All legendary entertainers have employed this technique at one time or another," David explains. Reveals allow the duo to introduce and directly play with influences on the collection. For the Spring/Summer 2014 "Space" show, in collaboration with Warner Bros., Phillipe emerged from a space suit in a direct riff on the opening credits from *Barbarella*, a camp cult-classic space odyssey starring Jane Fonda.

The Blonds consider the reveal from their jungle-inspired collection to be the most impactful. David says, "Phillipe opened the show to a very cinematic soundtrack and stripped out of a gorilla costume à la Marlene Dietrich in the 1932 film *Blonde Venus*, and then transformed the faux fur gorilla into a coat, live on the runway." The looks that followed evolved from researching the defense systems of various creatures, expressed in the garments through brightly colored materials, spikes, and large-scale feather sleeves.

The Blonds have always been committed to creating a safe space for inclusion and self-expression. Their shows are filled with exaggeration—colorful 1990s-inspired fantasies so camp that they may even border on fashion spoofs—but they always include an important message in the subtext.

Phillipe and David's shows are meant to inspire, titillate, entertain, and provide escape. There is always a little magic in the artifice of it all. And behind the magic, there's an army of people who make it all happen. "Our career has felt much like the story of *Alice in Wonderland* or *The Wizard of Oz*. Always filled with fantastic color and characters, the fashion world in and of itself can sometimes feel like a rollercoaster of dreams or the best film you've ever seen," David explains.

In this book, you'll learn some of the stories behind those shows, see The Blonds' favorite pieces, and catch a glimpse of never-before-seen moments from their career. Welcome to the world of The Blonds!

No
Business
Like
Show!

Always
look for
the
best one
at the
Blonds show!
The most
glamorous!
J'adore

- Carlyne Cerf
de Dudzeele

For Fall/Winter 2014 The Blonds drew inspiration from Catwoman, particularly Michelle Pfeiffer's incredible turn in *Batman Returns* (1992) as well as a scene out of *Ziegfeld Follies* (1945). Tim Burton's take on Batman features Selina Kyle's gloriously pink apartment, which she spraypaints black along with her cat t-shirt, translated here as a coat (above). The collection also reflects the movie's color palette and iconic weapons, including Catwoman's whip and retractable claws, modeled by Phillipe in his runway entrance (opposite).

Everything pretty
create's
meant
to make
the wearer
feel is
confident
and
powerful
as humanly
(or inhumanly)
possible
-Adam Lambert

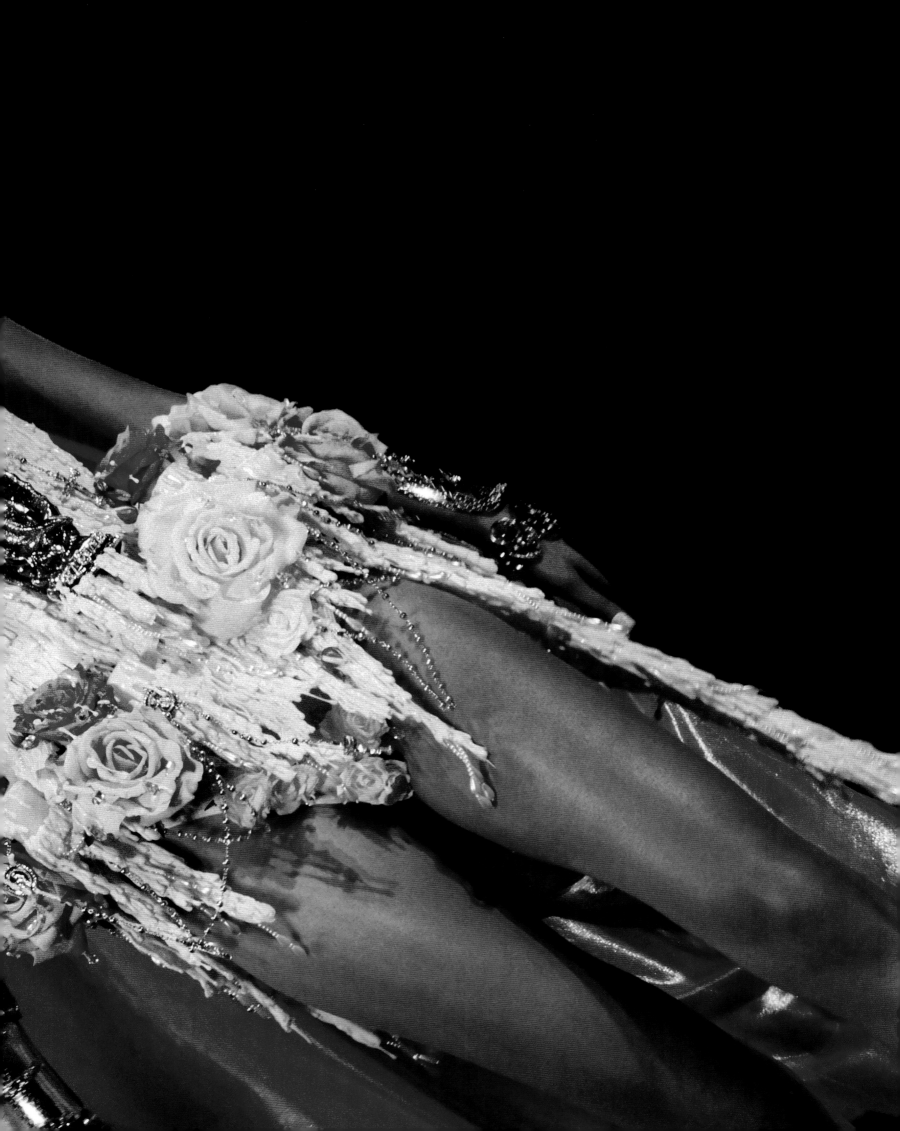

For The Blonds, watching *I Dream of Jeannie* was always the most fun. Spring/Summer 2015 saw the camp classic brought to life by mixing themes based in streetwear—a ribbed tank, buttoned shirts, jogging suits, *etc.*, with embelished religious and tattoo iconography as well as a nod to Marlene Dietrich's iconic dance scene in *Kismet* (1944).

We love The Blonds. David + Phillip Blond. They're so glamorous. We love them!

—Jennifer Saunders + Joanna Lumley

The Blonds make frequent references to Kubrick movies and rebelliously glamorous girl gangs. For Fall/Winter 2015 the collection and set were inspired by specific details from *A Clockwork Orange* (1971). The mannequins and masks used in the opening sequence (opposite) were actual molds of Phillipe's own body and face. The Blonds achieved this by working with Rootstein, the most celebrated mannequin designer and manufacturer in the world, to create mannequins that embodied both of Phillipe's personas.

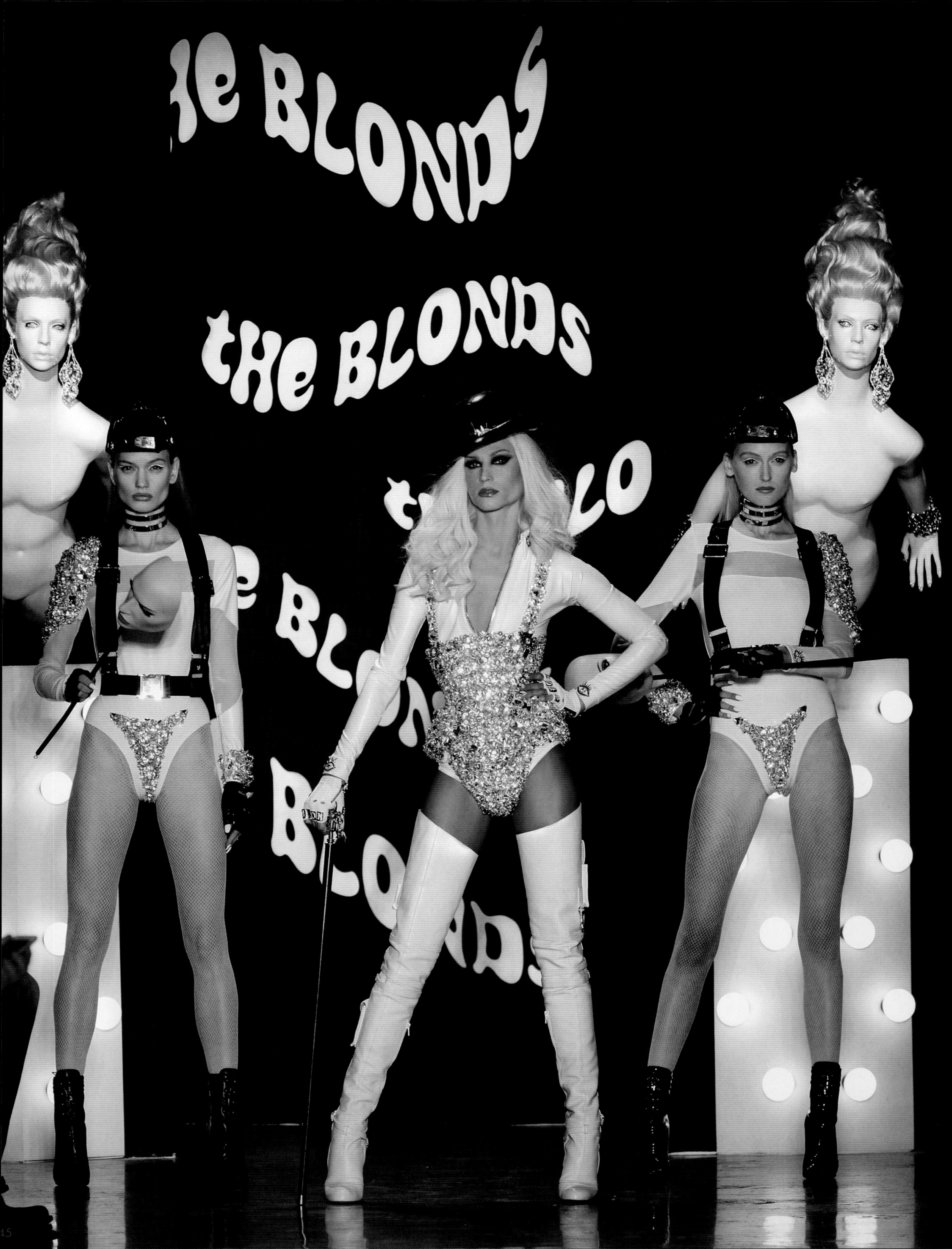
the BLONDS

MAZDACK RASSI
Co-Founder of MADE Fashion Week

Having The Blonds be a part of MADE Fashion Week is nothing short of revolutionary. We always include designers who are disrupting the status quo with their vision. There is no mistaking The Blonds' designs for anyone else's. Truly iconic!

One of The Blonds' favorite places to visit in New York is the Metropolitan Museum of Art, especially its extensive collection of Egyptian artifacts. The history and mythology behind burial ornamentation, as well as the way royalty lived as gods, obsessed with gold and the sun, were all inspirations for the Spring/Summer 2016 collection. The Blonds incorporated reptile and feather textures, a reflection of the Nile's crocodiles and ibises, and a bright blue color resembling Egyptian faience.

e forever fashion fantasy
air wildly theatrical runway
orld at each and every NYFW,
lor, courage, and unbridled
onds' unique and playful point
ry raison d'être—never fails to
d tantalize our imaginations.

MISS J. ALEXANDER

What do you get when you mix anticipation, corsets, beading, hair, nails, makeup, sky-high heels, six-foot models walking, music, screaming, clapping, crystals, and cheers during New York Fashion Week? The Blonds, that's what. Drag, drag, and more DRAG!

JAMES AGUIAR
Stylist

Part club, part circus, and all fashion, The Blonds systematically put on the greatest show of NYFW. Through the years they have consistently stuck to their vision and unapologetically served glitz and glamour down the throats of the fashion world's gaping mouths. Razzle and dazzle, fetish and frolic all come together in the perfect storm at any Blonds show.

TH

Greek Mythology,
constellations,
platinum, and
representation of
figures sculpted
in metal, clay
and stone

JENNÉ LOMBARDO
Co-Founder of MADE Fashion Week

To understand a Blonds show, you truly must attend one. It must be what it would have felt like to be at Studio 54 or inside a real-life music video. Now, if only I could get my waist as small as Phillipe's!

LAUREN EZERSKY
Host of Behind the Velvet Ropes

I wake up and think, how do I feel? Who am I today? And if I'm in the mood, I'll wear a ballgown to D'Agostino! Love The Blonds because they design clothes for the girl who *doesn't* live next door, and that's me!

NBC Universal partnered with The Blonds to promote *The Mummy* during Fall/Winter 2017 fashion week. The protagonist's narrative takes her from innocence, through vengeance, to immortal glory, which The Blonds interpreted through individual looks and in the show's sequence. Duality was a central theme: hard ornamentation on rich voluminous fabrics; soft textiles harnessed into structural pieces. Each piece reflected 1920s silhouettes, fabric treatments, and colors inspired by Erté.

From an early age, The Blonds
have loved performers
and performances —
this is the first thing
we found in common.
It is always great
fun and a huge
pleasure to collaborate
on their shows.
Long Live
The Blonds!
- Christian
Louboutin

The inspiration for Spring/Summer 2018 was twofold: music and Samuel Taylor Coleridge's depiction of Xanadu in his poem "Kubla Khan," apparently fueled by an opium dream. Musician Teyana Taylor, the muse for this collection, opened the show in a blue bodysuit and biker jacket (opposite). Reflective materials added shine to outfits that resembled the electric colors of birds of paradise. Tropical flowers and plants were also woven through the show: floral prints, flamingos, and wet hair looks with a hibiscus tucked behind the ear.

Opening the show was a highlight! It was yet another opportunity for us to rip apart the norms and up the status quo!
- Teyana Taylor

Quote by Teyana Taylor

"Kubla Khan" by Samuel Taylor Coleridge centers on an imperial "pleasure dome"; a place both beautiful & threatening. This collection also pays homage to musicians including ELVIS & 2PAC

This collection was inspired by Renaissance era frescoes, John Milton's Paradise Lost, Dante's Inferno, the early 1990's comic book character Lady Death and Kenneth Anger's Lucifer Rising.

Imagine Ursula, Maleficent, or Cruella De Vil as part of The Blonds' clientele. That was the brief from Disney when they entrusted The Blonds to design a collection around their most infamous characters. It didn't seem like a huge stretch: alter egos are often the core of fashion, after all.

As they mentally morphed these classic fictional villains into clients, they questioned, if designer Cruella De Vil were an entertainer in the real world, what would she wear on stage when performing? If the evil Queen, the antagonist from *Snow White and the Seven Dwarfs*, were to go out clubbing, how would she express her style? How would Maleficent dress for a gala if she wanted all eyes on her?

The answers, provided in the Spring 2019 collection, were a floor-length coat topped with black and white sequins that transform with a swipe of the hand, bodysuits covered in mirrored Perspex and golden beading, and an inky black corset embellished with Preciosa crystals and winding horns.

So much work goes into any show, but the Disney collection required additional research. Disney provided a list of all the villains, along with their signature descriptors and their individual mythologies. (For the show that would translate into every detail, including custom CND manicures, complete with feathers, hand-painted motifs, and, obviously, crystals for each character, as well as signature color combinations for each villain's liner and lipstick.) Typically, villains are meant to be secondary characters in most Disney films, but The Blonds believe they have the best style and the most personality and are the coolest characters.

"The evil Queen, Ursula, Cruella De Vil, Maleficent, Dr. Facilier, and the Queen of Hearts all have elaborate personal histories, and we loved digging in and learning about them. We traveled to the Walt Disney Animation Research Library in Glendale, California, to view the original sketches and sculpts behind each of the characters. We also had the incredible opportunity to see all the original artwork behind our favorite villains, as well as the process of animation past and present. For example, Ursula started off as a crayfish and went through different transformations until her creators had the idea of infusing the character with a bit of the personal style of drag artist Divine. That method of building a character is very similar to what we go through when crafting garments. We'll have one starting point, and then we'll build layers upon layers until in the end the garment has transformed into something completely different, but always fabulous!" recalls Phillipe.

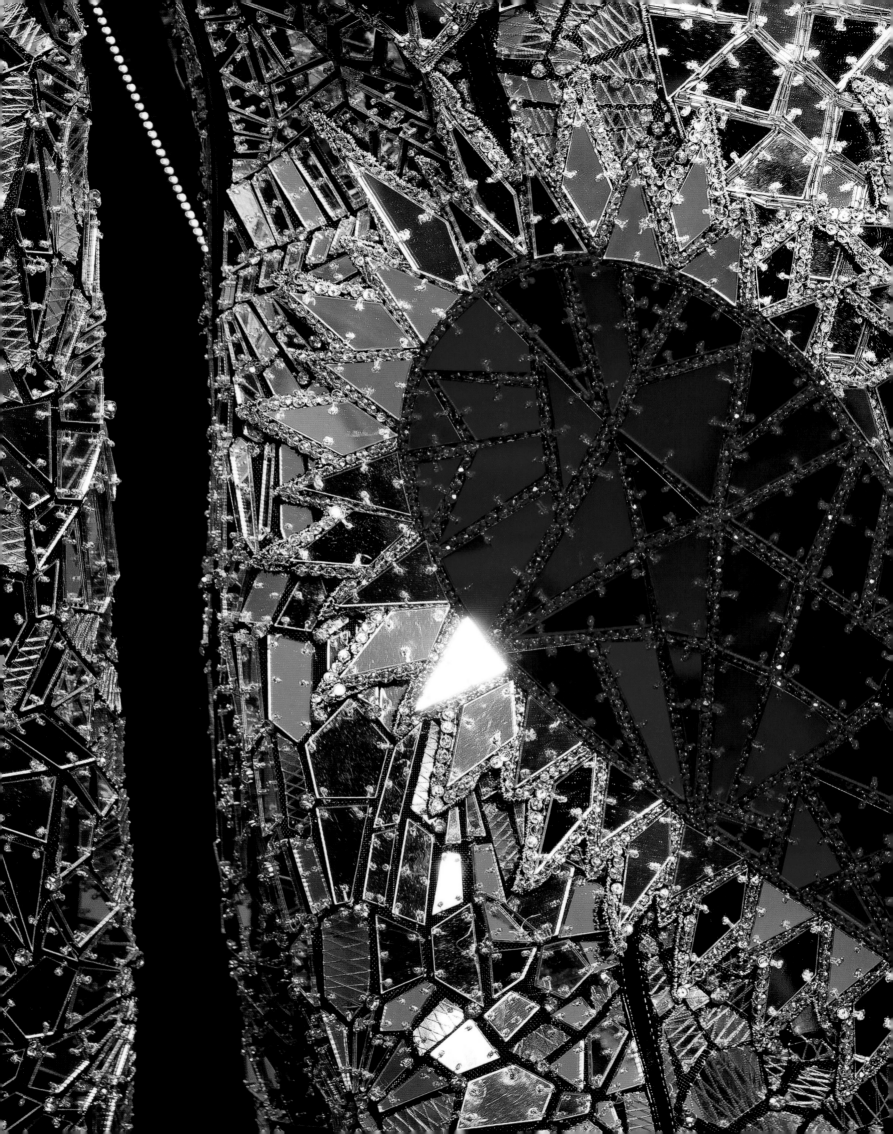

We wanted
the audience
to feel as if
Cruella de Vil
was out of
control and
speeding down
the runway
forward
them.

THE BLONDS

Quote by Dominique Jackson

THE

Dragons are the ultimate
symbol of power!
constructed of laser-cut
metallic scales. Phillipe's
Maleficent bodysuit gave
the illusion of being pierced
through the heart!

Once upon a Dream

NOAH KOZLOWSKI
Director of Global Designer Relations of IMG

Blonds shows are a personal New York Fashion Week highlight for me. There is an exciting energy in the room and the whole community comes out, blown away by the couture looks and next-level creativity.

There is nothing like a live event experience, which is why we continue presenting collections in a show format. The rise of digital media has attracted new consumers who not only follow the collections but want to shop the runway. This has given designers like The Blonds the opportunity to leverage their fashion shows as a form of cultural entertainment that helps them appeal to different audiences.

There are many considerations when recommending a designer for partnerships. That said, it took no time to come up with the idea of presenting The Blonds for these opportunities. Not only are they creative geniuses, but they're amazing humans—so easy to work with and admire. That's why they have cultivated such a strong community around them.

It was an honor to be a part of Disney's celebration of Mickey Mouse's 90th birthday and spin our own Blonds magic onto these iconic ears!

The Blonds' Fall/Winter 2019 collection, inspired by gangster films like *Casino* (1995) and *Scarface* (1983); featured jewel tones like emerald green combined with tiger prints, and glamorous golden hardware. Necklines plunged and shoulders expanded outward in a nod to film noir femmes fatales. Phillipe's entrance merged the style of Jerry Hall and Mr. T before the Clermont Twins, Karrueche Tran, Jillian Hervey, MJ Rodriguez, and Aquaria made appearances. Paris Hilton and Lil' Kim brought the house down for the finale!

I felt extremely sexy & edgy! The clothes literally feel like liquid gold on your body!
— MJ Rodriguez

I appreciate the creativity, playfulness & boldness in the actual pieces, but also in the energy they create for their shows.
—Jillian Hervey of Lion Babe

Who better
to perform
with than
the ultimate
friend:
Paris Hilton!
Kim
brought the
house down
with her hit
song "Jump Off"!

More is More is Better!

Their shows are like sitting front row at the most flashy concert imaginable
—Aquaria

Paris is a literal lifestyle, multifaceted like a diamond, and whenever we're together, it's like a supernova of sparkle, SLIVING!

Kim is an original, her incredibly unique sense of style is unmatched and we've shared some amazing moments together. We love Lil' Kim, she's the queen bee!

5

Sparkling Diamond!

The Blonds joined forces with the Tony award-winning *Moulin Rouge! The Musical* to celebrate the launch of their Spring 2020 collection and the official release of the original Broadway cast album. They worked very closely with celebrated producers Carmen Pavlovic, Bill Demaschke, choreographer Sonya Tayeh, as well as the teams at IMG, Endeavor, and Focus, led by Dominic Kaffka and Grace Rowe to merge Broadway and runway, creating a one-of-a-kind spectacle.

For one night only, the show was staged on the Broaway set of *Moulin Rouge! The Musical* at the Al Hirschfeld Theatre. The show featured the cast, including star Aaron Tveit, in a Preciosa-crystal-studded leather jacket, and special guests like fashion and theater impresario Jordan Roth. Phillipe descended from the ceiling, taking on the role of "the Sparkling Diamond," Paris Hilton flew across the stage to land on the Eiffel Tower, legendary dancer Leiomy Maldonado

vogued to tango as Tony, Grammy, Emmy-winner Billy Porter performed his hit single, "Love Yourself." For The Blonds, it was thrilling to bring the ultimate mashup of fashion, music, and theater to NYFW, culminating in the first-of-its-kind theatrical runway experience.

Music meant so much to the storytelling of this amazing production. The Blonds collaborated with renowned DJs, The Misshapes, Leigh Lezark and Geordon Nicol, to compose the complex soundtrack that combined elements of the live musical cast, film sound effects, pop, and everything in between. The Misshapes say: "producing show music for The Blonds is like soundtracking a mini feature film! David and Phillipe have a specific vision: over-the-top glamour, sex, drama, beauty, and love!"

Fern Mallis reminisces, "Clearly one of the highlights of attending NYFW is sitting front row at The Blonds. The only thing missing is

a cocktail in your hand. Being in their venue feels like being at the hottest club in New York. The audience represents every sector of the LGBTQIA+ community, as well as the coolest fashion editors, stylists, and celebrities. Then the show starts, and our jaws drop. The clothes are sexy, smart, flamboyant, and extraordinary. They are impeccably made and celebrate The Blonds' community. The clothes are not for everyone. They are meant for the stage and for very brave people who lead creative and free lives. The *Moulin Rouge* show was pure bliss, entertainment, and fabulous fashion. I didn't want it to end. No one but The Blonds could pull that off."

This show meant so much to The Blonds as fans, the honor of interpreting the world Baz Luhrmann and Catherine Martin created together. This show was dedicated to all those who believe in the power of love!

PARIS HILTON

Working with The Blonds is always a magical time! Everything they make is so beautiful, it's like a piece of art. Everything they've dressed me in is iconic. One of my favorite moments was their *Moulin Rouge* show, where I came out on the Eiffel Tower! From dressing as Cruella de Vil for their Disney show, to wearing a silvery crystal fringe bodysuit, every show has been so much fun. To sum it up, The Blonds are hot!

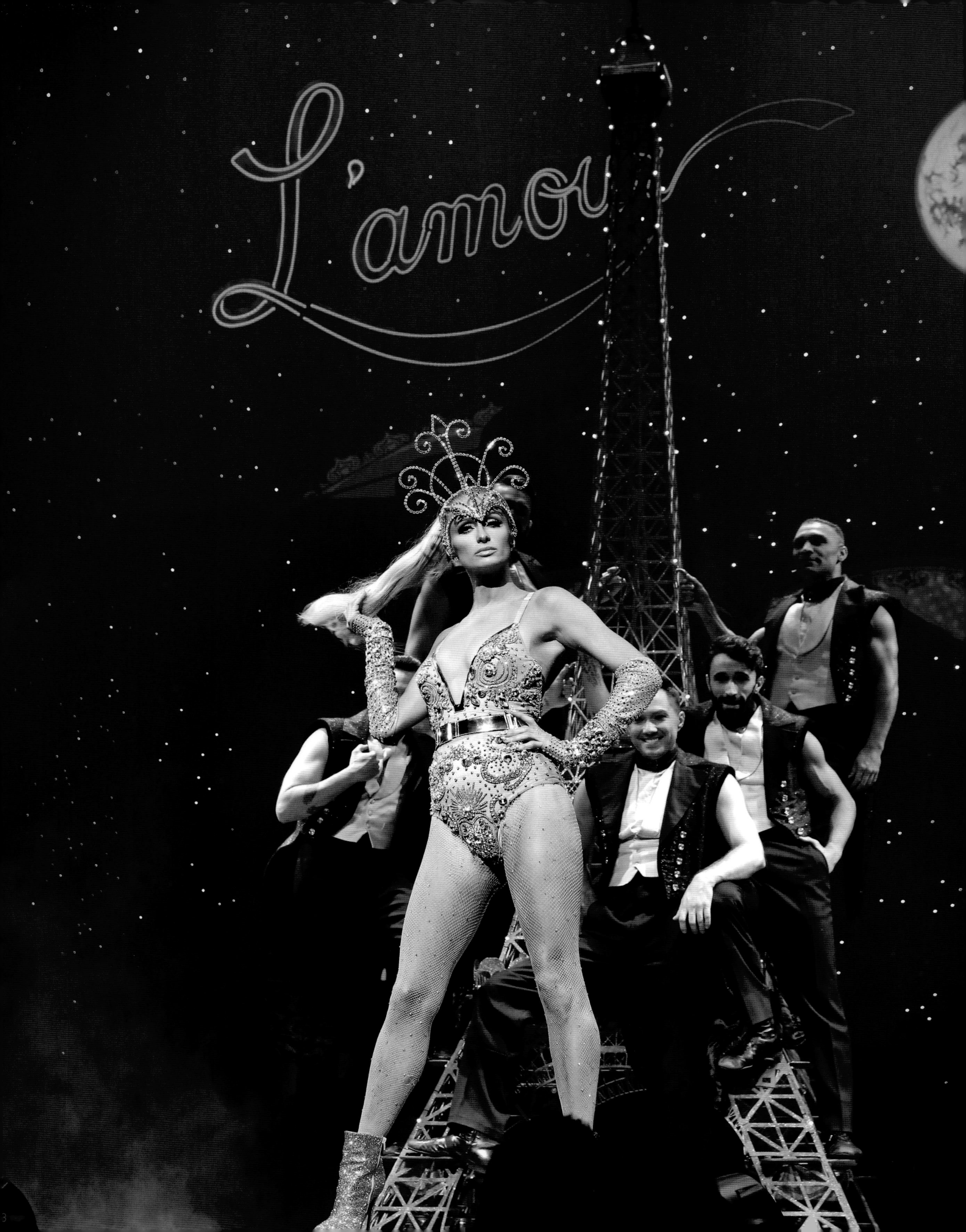
L'amou

Whenever I wear The Blonds I feel like the world is my BITCH!
— Gigi Gorgeous

The place where theater and fashion collide is the place of my fantasy —Jordan Roth

JILLIAN MERCADO

Representation is crucial for a society to move forward. My appearance in a Blonds show on February 9, 2020, instantly became an iconic part of the history of the runway. As a disabled Latinx queer woman, I was a pure representation of my multi-layered communities.

It was a moment for every person who has wanted to be seen and heard. It was for the countless times other people have spoken for us, not with us. It was a moment that The Blonds understood. Thank you to David and Phillipe for giving me this opportunity, a huge milestone in my career, and for understanding that everyone deserves to be included.

This moment was also brought to you by a young girl poring over magazines and watching fashion television while wondering whether the fashion world would accept her for who she was. She never saw anyone who had a visible disability in those magazines or on television.

I was invited to my first fashion show in 2012. That it was a show by The Blonds made it even more exciting. The line at the venue was around the block. Thankfully, a few people I knew from school were working the door and took me to my seat. From row six, the models on the runway looked tiny. As they walked, I thought, one day I'll be in the first row. Or better yet, in the show!

Every season I attended The Blonds' show and every season I was blown away by their amazing collections. On February 9, 2020, my fashion show experience came full circle. After attending the show year after year as a guest, I can now actually say I've been in the show. I can assure you this is only the beginning.

The Blonds summed up in one word: scintillating. Not only do their designs exude limitless sparkle, but they are also works of art. This is couture. This is theater. This is performance.

In 2019, I had worn a tuxedo gown to the Oscars, which garnered a fair amount of attention. When it was time for the Met Gala that year, I wanted to wear something not necessarily bigger, but wider in scope. The theme of that Met Gala was camp. There's a lot of misunderstanding about camp—people think it's kitschy or cheesy. Not so! Camp is a very high form of fashion—indeed, it is an art. It's the furthest you can go in your imagination. The Blonds understand that. Their work is very highly elevated camp with flawless construction.

Inspired by Diana Ross's Cleopatra moment during the montage in *Mahogany*, I had the notion of wearing something with an Egyptian influence that would tie into the Met's own impressive Egyptian collection. Not only was I familiar with the skills of The Blonds and their penchant for glitz and glamour, capes and bustiers, but I had been to their Fall 2019 show, a disco extravaganza. I knew The Blonds were the perfect choice for designing my ensemble.

Like all designers, The Blonds are also therapists and mind-readers. I just said, "Egyptian," and they came up with something I hadn't known I wanted until I saw it. They also have a way of folding you into their world until you find yourself doing things you never dreamed you'd do. They love catsuits. It's fair to say I was not a fan. I'd never even looked at a catsuit or considered wearing one.

Before I even knew what was happening, they had me happily ensconced in a catsuit. Their work is impeccable. Every fitting flowed with creative juices and excitement. They went over the outfit with a fine-toothed comb, making adjustments that were almost imperceptible to me, and fixing things I hadn't realized were off about the outfit.

"Outfit" is really a misnomer for their creation, which turned me into a dazzling fantasy creature, half Cleopatra and half Sun God. The Blonds garbed me in a bejeweled catsuit outfitted with enormous wings; a twenty-four-karat gold headpiece. I wore crystals and gold makeup. I was shimmering. I was borne into the building on a litter carried by six shirtless men. When I stepped off that litter and spread my ten-foot wings, I truly felt as if I could have soared into the sky.

I was sold on David and Phillipe's skills and abilities before working with them on this stunning project, but as we spent time together in advance of the 2019 Met Gala, I realized the most extraordinary thing about them: they're not only supremely talented, open, and collaborative, but they're also very, very kind. That was the cherry on top of the experience. It was such a joy to work with The Blonds, and the result was a moment the world will remember for a very long time.

Billy Porter
just made the
most fabulous
entrance in
Met Gala history.
— Vogue

Shooting Stars

Celine Dion completely
understands the value of
wearing something
impactful. She's one of
the only people Phillipe
would share a look with!

Living for Love!

The Blonds were asked to create a custom look for Madonna to be featured in her music video, "Living for Love." The creative aspects centered around the idea of an ultimate bullfighter. After researching the construction of a torero costume The Blonds noted it serves a purpose—the shoulder pads, fit, and stiffness of the bolero and suiting don't just create drama—they are meant to protect against the bull's horns! Additionally, the cape was cut and weighted to move a certain way on film.

The sheer black lace embroideries were very intricate, including crystallized roses. The materials were distressed by hand with an open flame to give the illusion of wear and tear. The roses express the tradition of tossing flowers on stage to show love, gratitude, and appreciation to the performer or artist.

B. Åkerland, Madonna's stylist, adds "The Blonds takes us into their dream world season after season, and my curiosity awaits their storytelling, ready to inhale the spirit of their magical fashion fantasy."

The Blonds continue, "Needless to say, this was a pinnacle for us as designers. Madonna represents so many things to us, and has always been inspiring. Getting to dress this queen was definitely magical! B. Åkerland lives and breathes fashion, our conversations and work together have always been an epic adventure."

This incredible outfit
felt I looked powerful
It fully came to life
with the movement
of a performance.
— Kylie Minogue

Kylie Minogue

Making a custom look for Miss Piggy was a page out of our dream book as kids. We fit this glamorous gown—based on Marilyn, of course—to create our version of Piggy Monroe. HI-YA!

The Blonds are on speed dial

— Rob & Mariel, stylists to JLo

65

The biggest musicians around the world look to David and Phillip for creative direction

— Jay Manuel

PATRICIA FIELD
Costume Designer

I met the Blonds when they walked into my shop Hotel Venus in SoHo, having just arrived from Florida. They showed me a pair of jeans on which they had stitched seashells and other ocean treasures. It was love at first sight. Their fantastic imagination struck me as a fashion explosion. They are truly an original and have maintained their image since day one.

The creations of The Blonds are so high fashion, eye-catching, and original that they are perfectly at home in TV and film, which rely heavily on visuals.

In the film *Sex and the City 2*, the girls go to a nightclub in the Middle East, where they are enticed into performing the song "I Am Woman." As soon as I read that scene in the script, I thought of this red Blonds dress with chains and spikes, as it perfectly matches Samantha's over-the-top personality.

Working with Kylie Minogue is electric and what designers' dreams are made of. Kylie has no boundaries where glamour is concerned, and neither does her creative director, William Baker: everything is possible! This corset is hand-draped in fine silk jersey, featuring a crystal-encrusted waist cincher with gold chain detail and cuffs. It was all inspired by Kylie's Aphrodite tour and the story of Andromeda.

Mariah is a fantasy

This power couple goes above Beyond to make the girls Shine Bright like Diamonds -Trina

Quote by Trina

5

I have so many great memories with them but my favorite has to be attending the show and then performing at their after party while pregnant with my princess. Royal

-Lil Kim

INDYA MOOR is Other worldly

The Blonds making into a mermaid's universe full of stars, or the most elegant gentleman in the world. They are Beauty quality creativity

-Gloria Trevi

This custom spiked corset is now housed in the Rock & Roll Hall of Fame. Rihanna won the American Music Awards that night.

Look at it! Come here, come a little closer, look at the detail. This shit is heavy, too, and when it's heavy, you know, it ain't cheap!

–Cardi B

Fireworks

Working with Katy Perry was one of the highlights of The Blonds' career, and probably the most fun because they were able to get away with almost anything! The sky was the limit and there were never boundaries. They transformed her into a modern-day showgirl, the Little Mermaid, and even Smurfette. David explains, "It was literally like waking up in Vegas over and over again!"

The 2011 "California Dreams" tour was huge and varied. The Blonds worked with Perry's stylist and costume designer Johnny Wujek to come up with some of her most iconic looks, including, in Phillipe's words, "this ultimate peppermint concoction that had rotating candy tits!"

The Blonds also developed a look inspired by Carmen Miranda (page 204) constructed of beaded fruit with crystal watermelon seed details. David continues, "This look meant a lot as it was her first time at the Grammys, and ours too." The Carmen Miranda dress is now a part of the permanent collection at the Grammy museum. Johnny explains "I always go to The Blonds when I need a showstopping costume made for my clients. They always serve up glitz and glam on the highest level! I have had so many amazing stage and carpet moments with The Blonds."

They're larger than life. I love that they have no limits!

— Katy Perry

Quote by Katy Perry

SUSANNE BARTSCH

Thank God for The Blonds! Without them I'd be
naked! I'd have to say, my style for going out
has always been about *showtime*, but fashion
evolved from the flash of the 1980s, when I
did more head-to-toe looks, to a more subdued
and eclectic feeling. The Blonds are completely
modern and forward thinking but retain that
element of drama that I love so much for my
usual nighttime high-drag looks. The Blonds'
body suits are to-die for—a must in any closet!
Bejeweled corsets have been staples of my
nocturnal looks since I started wearing Mr.
Pearl's creations. The Blonds have brought the
corset into now! The two words that sum up
drama, glamour, femme fatale sex, million
dollar babe: The Blonds.

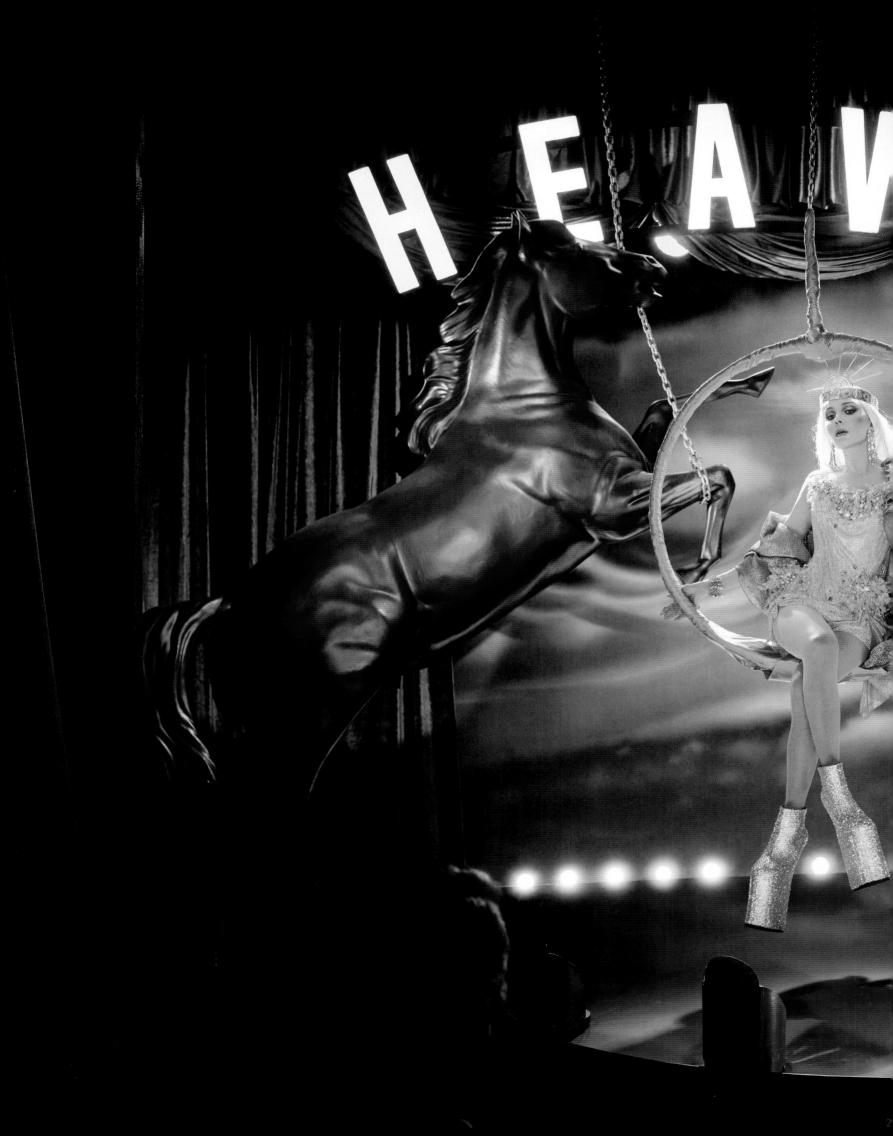

Everything we could hope & dream of! Stunning [signature]

Let's get Dirty!

The Blonds' vision brings such glamour and energy to the fashion world.
~ Gwen Stefani

Bangerz

Working on the Miley Cyrus "Bangerz" tour was like "being on a psychedelic drug," David explains. Every element maximized color, sparkle, and scale to create a sensory overload. It transported the audience to a place that was one part rock concert, and one part *The Ren & Stimpy Show*.

The looks on pages 231 and 233 were called the "mouth monsters," and were meant to be crystallized exaggerations of Miley's famous mouth, which was also incorporated into the set design. At one point Miley entered the stage on a tongue slide. Padded fabric provided dimensional structure and protection for her lip jacket.

This bejeweled pot print was for her "Love, Money, Party" segment. Simone Harouche, Cyrus' stylist for the Bangerz tour, explains The Blonds are "the first designers I think of when I think of performance looks. Their pieces are made for the stage!"

EVERY CENT OF THE SELLING PRICE OF VIVA GLAM LIPSTICK AND LIPGLASS IS DONATED TO THE M·A·C AIDS FUND TO SUPPORT MEN, WOMEN AND CHILDREN LIVING WITH HIV AND AIDS WWW.MACCOSMETICS.COM

Designing for Barbie was a childhood dream come true for David and Phillipe. The duo had previously worked on several one-of-a-kind dolls and other projects with Mattel before they received a commission to create two of their own.

For The Blonds' Diamond Barbie (pages 246–247), the designers worked to create a look that expressed strength, power, beauty, and glamour. The design process was unusually challenging, as every detail needed to be miniaturized. The Blonds worked with Bill Greening and the team at Mattel to push the boundaries, "The diamond look was inspired by Phillipe's personal style—Barbie was in drag for the first time!" David explains. This in turn influenced the full-sized look worn by Dominique Jackson on page 248.

For the their gold Barbie, the process was again challenging, as everything had to be custom-made. The Blonds had the body position custom cast, as well as the spike ring, cuffs, and shoes. The corset itself had real gold chain details. The stand was intended to reflect a cross between gold bullion and Superman's ice castle. David explains "This particular look was very special to us, as we had recently created something similar for Kylie Minogue, now immortalized on Barbie."

What a dream to
have been dressed
by The Blonds!
From someone
who loves
glamour, I just
can't get
enough of
their rock star
sparkle and
dazzle and
I couldn't dress.
adore it more!

Barbie

Making
Magic!

KABUKI
Key Makeup Artist, MAC Cosmetics

Makeup plays a major role in continuing the narrative of a look, or in the case of a show, an entire collection. Simply put, if you look at a photo or even a drawing of a person, you will immediately look at their face for some clues about them. It's the perfect opportunity to include details and touches that subliminally affect how the whole look is presented. The most exciting thing about doing The Blonds' shows is feeling the energy from the models as they start the lineup. By then, they feel totally transformed from who they were when they walked in and sat in the makeup chair.

The Blonds usually have an abundance of makeup ideas. It's about editing down to the essentials and honing the details. The makeup design has to tell a narrative and also look right as a consistent element in the show. Even though every season's makeup is different, there are signature elements to a Blonds makeup look: Streamlined eyes, a sculpted bone structure and glowy highlights, a tricolor contoured lip, slightly overdrawn at the upper edge, a groomed brow, full-body makeup so you pop in the light.

Sometimes we've extended the ornamentation of the look by adding appliqué elements to the makeup. Gold Mylar tears for Genie, hand-cut gold Mylar eyeliner and a full Eye of Horus for Egyptian Disco. Each made the night before the show by yours truly!

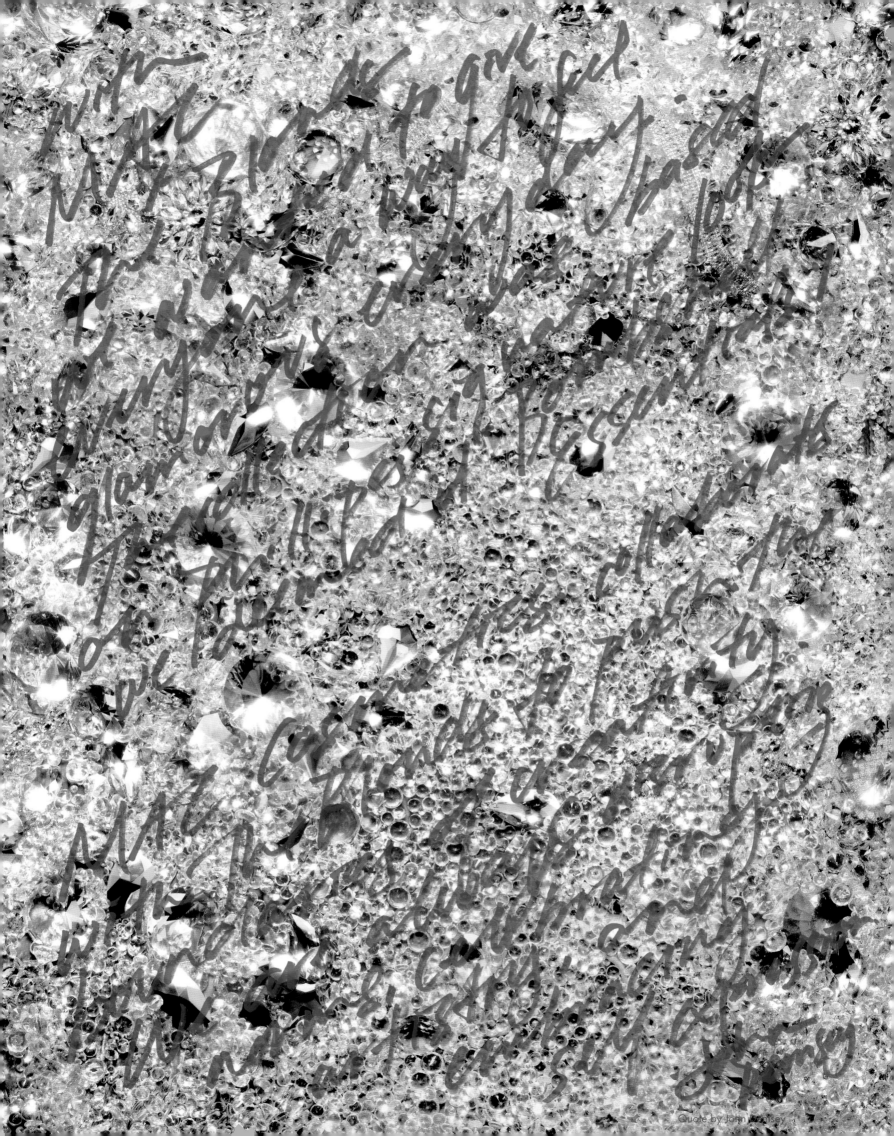

HOW IT'S MADE

The muse for each piece in a collection can be almost anything—a striking image, a bright color or even a sound. The Blonds build from there to create a mood or attitude and begin to sketch. As development continues, the pre-production process begins with sourcing of fabric swatches, treatments, creation of embroidery, bead, and crystal material samples. All of these elements come together to begin creating the look and feel of a garment. Toiles are then made to develop construction and silhouettes. The final garments are created using different techniques, which vary depending on the collection's theme.

For a custom garment, the demands of the show or client dictate the approach. Sometimes there are several fittings and the pieces are worked on by multiple people, until they are finally detailed in The Blonds' studio to completion.

Other elements are coded into The Blonds' brand signature. Metal materials like chains, and mesh fabrics are sometimes used exclusively or mixed with multiple shapes to create a clash of textures. Of course Preciosa crystals are The Blonds' favorite thing to use and "add the most excitement," according to David. "Sparkle makes everything feel dream-like, and when worn, feels like a transformative experience."

For the Blonds, spikes and studs instantly give an edge to a garment. The designers use them on everything from traditional leather to fabrics like lace and satin, and are perhaps the first designers to popularize merging spikes with crystal elements. David concludes, "Experimenting with new and different ways to use a material is one of the things that keeps us inspired."

JAN ARNOLD
Co-Founder and Style Director of CND Nails

We are a match made in heaven! The Blonds understand the role of nails as an accessory and use them to punctuate looks on the runway. We realized that their atelier looked like ours, only we work in miniature, on the tiny canvas of a nail. Over the fifteen years we've worked together, we've developed a language for nails that helps us to fuel each other's creativity.

Nails are the punctuation mark for a look. They can communicate the alter-ego of the wearer; they can bridge feminine and masculine; they can be a high contrast accessory; and they can even become a theater for artistic expression. Because nails adorn the digits of hands, and hands express, a nail can even change the attitude or posture of the wearer. They add length to the silhouette of the hand and lend excitement and reinforcement to other elements.

The fashion story indicates the attitude of the nail, e.g., glamour, classic, punk, or downtown. The fabric gives direction on color, dimension, and opacity. The silhouette gives the nail shape and length needed. For The Blonds, the look is always fierce and illuminated with shine and richness. The CND Design Lab use thousands of crystals for a single set of nails, all handcrafted by artisans from around the world!

KEVIN HUGHES
Artistic Director of Moroccanoil

Hair tells part of the story. In fashion, the hair is often minimized so that it does not detract from the clothing. But that is where The Blonds are different. They know hair is part of that character, which in turn is part of their vision. They don't worry about hair taking over a look, but rather they make the hair a part of the look. It is like any other accessory—the most important accessory because you don't take it off. Well, unless it's a wig!

As an artist, I am always searching for inspiration, and you cannot see a Blonds show without being inspired. Whether for NYFW or for the images in this spread, David and Phillipe always explain their direction in detail. I love that because I can envision it all before it comes together. The model must become that vision. David and Phillipe really look to other artists for their opinions and listen to what we have to say.

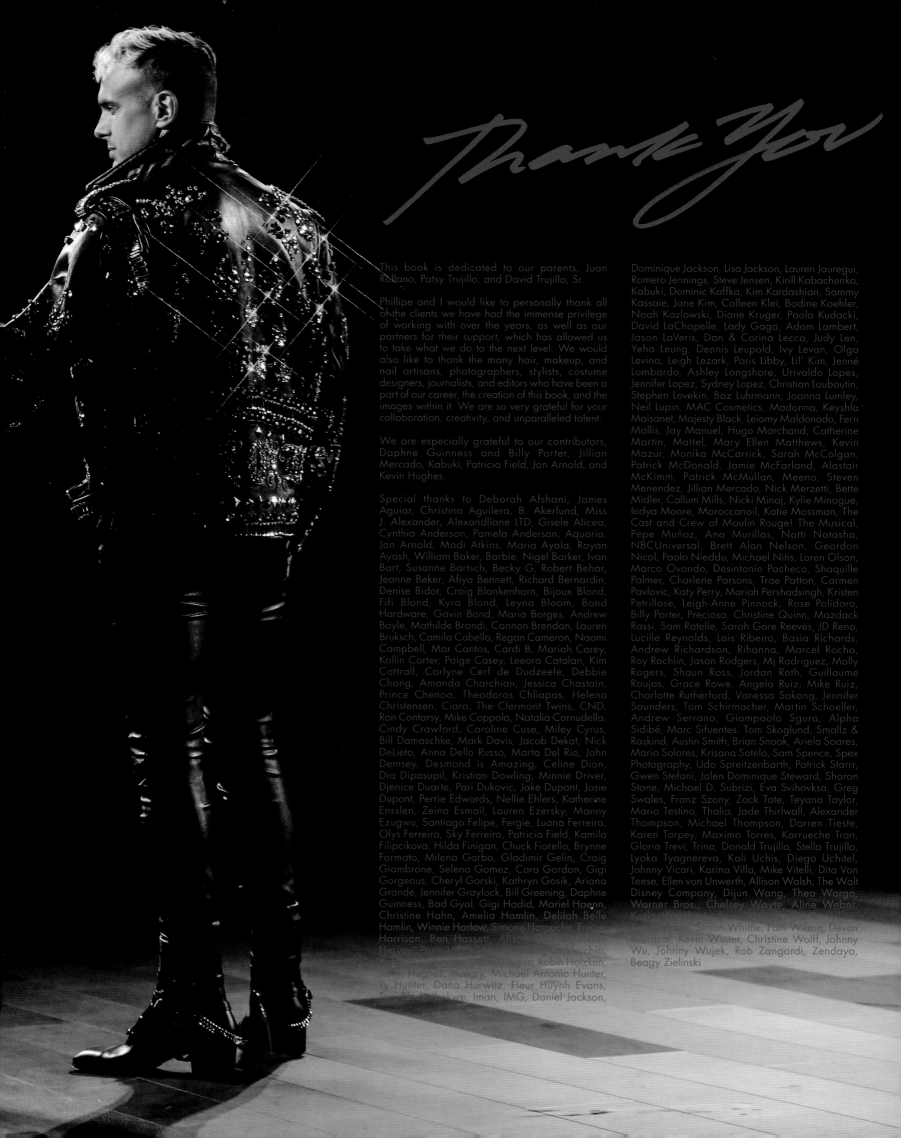

Thank You

This book is dedicated to our parents, Juan Rollano, Patsy Trujillo, and David Trujillo, Sr.

Phillipe and I would like to personally thank all of the clients we have had the immense privilege of working with over the years, as well as our partners for their support, which has allowed us to take what we do to the next level. We would also like to thank the many hair, makeup, and nail artisans, photographers, stylists, costume designers, journalists, and editors who have been a part of our career, the creation of this book, and the images within it. We are so very grateful for your collaboration, creativity, and unparalleled talent.

We are especially grateful to our contributors, Daphne Guinness and Billy Porter, Jillian Mercado, Kabuki, Patricia Field, Jan Arnold, and Kevin Hughes.

Special thanks to Deborah Afshani, James Aguiar, Christina Aguilera, B. Akerlund, Miss J. Alexander, Alexandliane LTD, Gisele Alicea, Cynthia Anderson, Pamela Anderson, Aquaria, Jan Arnold, Madi Atkins, Maria Ayala, Rayan Ayash, William Baker, Barbie, Nigel Barker, Ivan Bart, Susanne Bartsch, Becky G, Robert Behar, Jeanne Beker, Afiya Bennett, Richard Bernardin, Denise Bidot, Craig Blankenhorn, Bijoux Blond, Fifi Blond, Kyra Blond, Leyna Bloom, Bond Hardware, Gavin Bond, Maria Borges, Andrew Boyle, Mathilde Brandi, Cannon Brendan, Lauren Bruksch, Camila Cabello, Regan Cameron, Naomi Campbell, Mar Cantos, Cardi B, Mariah Carey, Kollin Carter, Paige Casey, Leeora Catalan, Kim Cattrall, Carlyne Cerf de Dudzeele, Debbie Chang, Amanda Charchian, Jessica Chastain, Prince Chenoa, Theodoros Chliapas, Helena Christensen, Ciara, The Clermont Twins, CND, Ron Contarsy, Mike Coppola, Natalia Cornudella, Cindy Crawford, Caroline Cuse, Miley Cyrus, Bill Damaschke, Mark Davis, Jacob Dekat, Nick DeLieto, Anna Dello Russo, Marta Del Rio, John Demsey, Desmond is Amazing, Celine Dion, Dia Dipasupil, Kristian Dowling, Minnie Driver, Djenice Duarte, Pari Dukovic, Jake Dupont, Josie Dupont, Perrie Edwards, Nellie Ehlers, Katherine Ensslen, Zeina Esmail, Lauren Ezersky, Manny Ezugwu, Santiago Felipe, Fergie, Luana Ferreira, Olys Ferreira, Sky Ferreira, Patricia Field, Kamila Filipcikova, Hilda Finigan, Chuck Fiorello, Brynne Formato, Milena Garbo, Gladimir Gelin, Craig Giambrone, Selena Gomez, Cara Gordon, Gigi Gorgeous, Cheryl Gorski, Kathryn Gosik, Ariana Grande, Jennifer Graylock, Bill Greening, Daphne Guinness, Bad Gyal, Gigi Hadid, Mariel Haenn, Christine Hahn, Amelia Hamlin, Delilah Belle Hamlin, Winnie Harlow, Simone Harouche, Erica Harrison, Ben Hassett, Alison Hernon, Jillian Hervey, Paris Hilton, Courtney Hoffman, Hair by Hollywood, Jeremy Scott Logan, Robin Holzken, Kevin Hughes, Hungry, Michael Antonio Hunter, Ty Hunter, Dana Hurwitz, Fleur Huynh Evans, Toni Akinotholwe, Iman, IMG, Daniel Jackson,

Dominique Jackson, Lisa Jackson, Lauren Jauregui, Romero Jennings, Steve Jensen, Kirill Kabachenko, Kabuki, Dominic Kaffka, Kim Kardashian, Sammy Kassaie, Jane Kim, Colleen Klei, Bodine Koehler, Noah Kozlowski, Diane Kruger, Paola Kudacki, David LaChapelle, Lady Gaga, Adam Lambert, Jason LaVeris, Dan & Corina Lecca, Judy Len, Yeha Leung, Dennis Leupold, Ivy Levan, Olga Levina, Leigh Lezark, Paris Libby, Lil' Kim, Jenné Lombardo, Ashley Longshore, Urivaldo Lopes, Jennifer Lopez, Sydney Lopez, Christian Louboutin, Stephen Lovekin, Baz Luhrmann, Joanna Lumley, Neil Lupin, MAC Cosmetics, Madonna, Keyshla Maisonet, Majesty Black, Leiomy Maldonado, Fern Mallis, Jay Manuel, Hugo Marchand, Catherine Martin, Mattel, Mary Ellen Matthews, Kevin Mazur, Monika McCarrick, Sarah McColgan, Patrick McDonald, Jamie McFarland, Alastair McKimm, Patrick McMullan, Meeno, Steven Menendez, Jillian Mercado, Nick Merzetti, Bette Midler, Callum Mills, Nicki Minaj, Kylie Minogue, Indya Moore, Moroccanoil, Katie Mossman, The Cast and Crew of Moulin Rouge! The Musical, Pepe Muñoz, Ana Murillas, Natti Natasha, NBCUniversal, Brett Alan Nelson, Geordon Nicol, Paolo Nieddu, Michael Nitis, Loren Olson, Marco Ovando, Desintonio Pacheco, Shaquille Palmer, Charlene Parsons, Trae Patton, Carmen Pavlovic, Katy Perry, Mariah Pershadsingh, Kristen Petrillose, Leigh-Anne Pinnock, Rose Polidoro, Billy Porter, Preciosa, Christine Quinn, Mazdack Rassi, Sam Ratelle, Sarah Gore Reeves, JD Reno, Lucille Reynolds, Lais Ribeiro, Basia Richards, Andrew Richardson, Rihanna, Marcel Rocha, Roy Rochlin, Jason Rodgers, Mj Rodriguez, Molly Rogers, Shaun Ross, Jordan Roth, Guillaume Roujas, Grace Rowe, Angela Ruiz, Mike Ruiz, Charlotte Rutherford, Vanessa Sakong, Jennifer Saunders, Tom Schirmacher, Martin Schoeller, Andrew Serrano, Giampaolo Sgura, Alpha Sidibé, Marc Sifuentes, Tom Skoglund, Smallz & Raskind, Austin Smith, Brian Snook, Ariela Soares, Mario Solares, Krisana Sotelo, Sam Spence, Spex Photography, Udo Spreitzenbarth, Patrick Starrr, Gwen Stefani, Jalen Dominique Steward, Sharon Stone, Michael D. Subrizi, Eva Svihovksa, Greg Swales, Franz Szony, Zack Tate, Teyana Taylor, Mario Testino, Thalia, Jade Thirlwall, Alexander Thompson, Michael Thompson, Darren Tieste, Karen Torpey, Maximo Torres, Karrueche Tran, Gloria Trevi, Trina, Donald Trujillo, Stella Trujillo, Lyoka Tyagnereva, Kali Uchis, Diego Uchitel, Johnny Vicari, Karina Villa, Mike Vitelli, Dita Von Teese, Ellen von Unwerth, Allison Walsh, The Walt Disney Company, Dijun Wang, Theo Wargo, Warner Bros., Chelsey Wayte, Aline Weber, Karla Welch, Simon Whittle, Patti Wilson, Devon Windsor, Kevin Winter, Christine Wolff, Johnny Wu, Johnny Wujek, Rob Zangardi, Zendaya, Beagy Zielinski

CRYSTALS BY
PRECIOSA